"The developmental needs of young adolescents are very real, yet it is often difficult to find youth ministry materials specifically geared to their age level, especially in the area of spirituality. Gwen Costello's book, *Prayer Services for Young Adolescents*, fills this vacuum in a very meaningful way. Her choice of topics for prayer are 'right on' and 'right where' the young teenager is; they reveal a personal acquaintance with this age group. And her methodology, especially the guided meditations, are to me so well chosen...in my experience these are the ways that young people enjoy praying the best!"

Joe Moore
New England Consultants

"Gwen Costello has done catechists and young adolescents (as well as their parents) an immense favor by producing this book. The prayer services offer young people the opportunity to face their concerns in the presence of God and deal with them. Each service includes a variety of prayer forms: scripture reading, guided meditation, choral prayer, silent prayer, and an engaging activity. The topics are right on target. This book is an appealing, powerful means for youth to form values—something sorely needed today."

Mary Kathleen Glavich, SND
General Editor, *Christ Our Life* series
(Loyola University Press)

"Gwen Costello has provided an invaluable resource with *Prayer Services for Young Adolescents*. Not only does the book provide wonder-filled ideas for prayer with 'Quicksilvers' (young adolescents), it also has some important insights into what makes young adolescents 'tick.' This book is an excellent tool for catechists, youth ministers, teachers, and parents."

Carole D. Goodwin
Author, *Quicksilvers: Ministering With Junior High Youth*

"*Prayer Services for Young Adolescents* is a must for those who want to help young adolescents pray. The topics are timely: sexuality, self-awareness, clothes, language, friends, etc. The services are alive with the urgency, dynamism, and counter-cultural values of the gospel of Christ. The young are invited to pray with scripture, to pray with guided meditation, with silence, and with choral responses. The clear directions and well-ordered format make this book very easy to use. Gwen Costello's experience as a Christian educator and her love for the young inform every page."

Kevin Regan
Author, *More Prayer Services for Teens*

GWEN COSTELLO

PRAYER SERVICES
for Young Adolescents

TWENTY-THIRD PUBLICATIONS
Mystic, CT 06355

Second printing 1995

Twenty-Third Publications
185 Willow Street
P.O. Box 180
Mystic, CT 06355
(203) 536-2611
800-321-0411

© Copyright 1994 Gwen Costello. All rights reserved.
These services work best when each participant has a copy, so permission is granted to duplicate copies, as needed, for non-commercial use in schools, churches, and for other prayer groups. Otherwise, no part of this publication may be reproduced in any manner without prior written permission of the publisher. Write to Permissions Editor.

ISBN 0-89622-597-6
Library of Congress Catalog Card Number 94-60311
Printed in the U.S.A.

Dedication

For Kevin Costello
and adolescents everywhere
who are trying to:
grow in self-esteem,
love and respect others,
and deepen their faith in God.

This is my prayer for you:
"May your love keep on growing
more and more,
together with true knowledge
and perfect judgment
so that you will always be able
to choose what is right" (Phil 1:9–10).

TABLE OF CONTENTS

Introduction — 1

1. We Are What We Are — 4
Young adolescents tend to focus on their negative qualities and to wish they were different or better. This service encourages them to be grateful for the gift of themselves and to accept themselves as God made them.

2. Lost in the Crowd — 8
Moving into new groups and feeling comfortable within existing groups is a real challenge for many young adolescents. This service suggests ways they can relate to peers with love and respect.

3. Life Is Not Fair — 12
Some adolescents are outgoing and others simply are not. This service emphasizes the importance of recognizing and accepting their own particular gifts and talents.

4. Lighten Up! — 16
Many young adolescents are uptight about everything they do and say, believing that everyone is watching and judging them. This service encourages them to be comfortable with themselves so that they will be more comfortable with and accepting of others.

5. Everybody Does It — 20
Because peer pressure is so difficult to avoid, many young adolescents begin bad habits like smoking, drinking, or using drugs. This service emphasizes the importance of avoiding these habits and of forming good habits, in spite of what everyone else is doing.

6. A Few Good Friends — 24
Many young people abandon true friends to follow a more popular person or crowd. This service describes some of the attributes of real friendship and emphasizes the importance of valuing and affirming friends.

7. Accentuate the Positive — 28
When young adolescents compare themselves to others, they tend to focus on their negative attributes. This service reminds them that they can't be compared to anyone else because they are unique.

8. What About Sex?   33
Young adolescents often confuse sexuality with sexual acts. This service emphasizes sexuality as a special gift from God that helps them relate to others. It points out the difference between being a sexual person and engaging in sexual acts.

9. What's Wrong With Swearing?   38
Adolescents often resort to swearing, ranking on others, and belittling others with language in order to make themselves look good. This service stresses the importance of affirming others through positive language and of avoiding the habit of swearing.

10. Who Should We Follow?   43
Young adolescents are under tremendous pressure today to follow people whose lives are examples of greed, immorality, and godlessness. They need people in their lives to counteract these messages. This service assures them that the message of Jesus, though difficult, is the true one. It points the way to God.

11. Clothes Make the Person   48
Consumerism is one of the greatest temptations of young adolescence. Our culture, especially through the media, bombards them with the message that happiness is equal to more and more possessions. This service invites them to look around and focus on the many beautiful things they already have—especially little things.

12. There's a World Out There   53
Being self-absorbed is typical for young adolescents, and thus they need encouragement to reach out to others. This service reminds them that many others around them are needy, and that they can reach out in love and service.

13. Why Parents Make You Do It   58
Because young adolescents face so many obstacles and struggles, they need spiritual guidance and nourishment. This service points out how the Mass, sacraments, and other forms of ritual prayer can strengthen and guide them.

14. Is There Really a God?   63
Even as young adolescents practice their faith, they still have nagging doubts about God. This service encourages them to believe—without proof—that God through and in Jesus is always with them to guide and strengthen them in the growing-up process.

Appendix One   67

Appendix Two   70

Introduction

I never attended "middle school" or "junior high." Those grades for me were simply extensions of what preceded them. St. Mary's School in Laurel, Maryland, had eight classrooms and eight grades. There was no kindergarten, no gym, no music or art rooms, and certainly no middle school—just eight very crowded classrooms. Young adolescents today fare better in terms of space, numbers in a class, and special activities. But one thing remains the same: human nature. Even in my very crowded sixth, seventh, and eighth grade classrooms, it was always clear who the popular kids were, who wore the right clothes, who lived in the best houses, and so on. Putting down and/or excluding those who didn't fit such criteria was standard fare.

Today's better learning environment has not guaranteed mutual respect, acceptance, courtesy, or cooperation among our young adolescents. They still reject those who are different, "rank" on one another, exclude those who are at the edge, compete with one another, verbally assault one another—and sometimes even physically bully and batter one another.

Any of us who have worked with young adolescents know that this is so. We also know that many young people today are sometimes rude and uncooperative not just with one another, but also toward parents, teachers, and other adults. We know, too, that this rudeness is apt to contain expletives. I can't imagine ever having said "damn"—much less some of the saltier language catechists and teachers hear today—in the presence of Sister Callista or Sister Pulcheria!

WHY this is so is material for another book, but THAT it is so is why I have written these prayer services. I am convinced that our young adolescents today will benefit immensely from learning—or relearning—Christian values, beginning with the most basic value of all: "Love one another as I have loved you."

Love involves caring, listening, respecting, affirming, and cooperating, and these are the themes of these fourteen services. Each offers young adolescents (sixth through ninth graders) opportunities to reflect, pray, and respond to one another and to God. Each addresses problems and concerns that are directly affecting them today, but always in the context of growing in mutual respect for themselves and others.

How to Use These Services
They can be used as opening or closing prayers for your regular classes, but note that they take twelve minutes or so if done in their entirety (which I hope you'll consider time well spent). They can also be used during retreats or on days or evenings of reflection. Since the themes are not seasonal, they can be used at any time of year. They do not have to be used in the order in which they appear in this book. Indeed, there may be times when your group is in particular need of one topic more than others, so feel free to use the service that is most appropriate for your own situation at any given time.

Each service has six components: 1) opening prayer, 2) scripture reading, 3) guided meditation, 4) group response, 5) silent personal prayer, and 6) group closing prayer. You are free, of course, to use only parts of each service if your time is restricted. For example, if you can only allot five minutes to class prayer, use the opening prayer, allow time for silent reflection, and conclude with the group closing prayer. Or use the scripture reading, the guided meditation, and conclude with moments of silent prayer.

I highly recommend that you always precede your prayer time with brief moments of lively and friendly interaction among participants. In other words, don't enter prayer experiences "cold." Help your young adolescents warm up to one another and to you through "icebreakers." These need not be complex and should only take a few minutes. A little fun goes a long way. (See Appendix One on page 67 for suggestions.) Remember that even our prayer times together should be a joy and a delight because we are celebrating something great—the presence of our God among us.

Note that in Appendix Two (on page 70), you will find advice about how to introduce participants to guided meditation. If your group is unfamiliar with this process, you will want to review this information before leading them in this form of prayer. I also recommend that after the prayer service you allow time for participants to talk about what they experienced during these meditations—*if they want to*. Some prefer not to discuss what happened to them, but others can't wait to do so. This is something you have to gauge by knowing your own group, but offering the opportunity is important for those who do want to share their experiences.

No matter how you use these services, the important thing is that they encourage your young adolescents to get comfortable with themselves, to reflect on their attitudes toward one another, and to respond to their Christian call to follow Jesus who shows them the way to God.

SERVICE ONE

We Are What We Are

Note for Leader: Young adolescents tend to focus on their negative qualities, wishing they were different or better. This service encourages them to be grateful for the gift of themselves and to accept themselves as God made them. You will need a prayer table on which is placed a bible (open to Genesis 1:26–31), a candle, and a mirror. (Optional: Have small mirrors, one for each participant, to distribute at the end of the service.) Assign pray-ers and readers and then open the service gathered in a circle around your prayer table.

Opening Prayer

Leader: Hello, God.
We are here to talk to you for a while,
and to think about your place in our lives.

Pray-er One: When we were younger
we learned that you made us
and that everything you made is good.
We want to believe this,
but we sometimes find it hard
to accept ourselves *as good*.

Pray-er Two: We want to be better, smarter,
different, more popular, taller,
shorter, smaller, heavier, more outgoing,
less talkative, and happier,
but *we are what we are*.

---

4 Reprinted with permission from *Prayer Services for Young Adolescents* by Gwen Costello
© 1994 Twenty-Third Publications, P.O. Box 180, Mystic, CT 06355 (800-321-0411).

Pray-er Three: Help us during this prayer time
to understand a little better
how to appreciate ourselves
and to know that we are good
—just as you have made us.
Amen.

Scripture Reading (Genesis 1:26–31 paraphrased)

Leader: *God made us as we are, and though it may be
difficult for us to see ourselves as good,
this reading assures us that we are.*

Reader One: God said,
"Let us make the man and woman
in our own image, in the likeness of ourselves,
and let them be partners of the fish of the sea,
the birds of heaven, the cattle, all the wild beasts,
and all the reptiles that crawl upon the earth."

Reader Two: God created them
and they were indeed very much like God,
male and female God created them.

Reader Three: God blessed them, saying to them...
"See, I give you plants and trees with fruit..."
And so it was.
God looked over everything that had been made,
especially the man and woman,
and saw that indeed it was very good.
The Word of the Lord.

All: Thanks be to God.

Guided Meditation

Leader: Close your eyes and slowly breathe in and out. Do this several times. ...*pause.* Now imagine that you are walking on a road and as you walk along you suddenly remember that you are looking for something. The only clue you have is that the object is in a garden. Up ahead you see a wooden fence and you quickly climb over it. It's the garden! Picture it in your mind. ...*pause.*

You start down the first row looking for the object, and then you go down row after row. ...*pause*. Finally you see something shiny and you bend down and pick up a key. This is what you were looking for, but you don't know what it opens.

But then you see a farmer coming toward you with a box. She smiles and hands you the box. "This is yours," she says; "it's a gift from God." Quickly you put the key in the lock and open the box. You lift the gift out and look at it. It's a mirror! What kind of gift is this? Why would God give you a mirror?...*pause*.

(After 30 seconds or so, invite participants to open their eyes.)

Group Response

Leader: What do we see when we look in a mirror?
Ourselves. Only ourselves.
Let us thank and praise God for the gift of ourselves.

Left Side: God, you look at me and you see that I am good.

Right Side: Help me to see the good that you see.

Left Side: All I see are my defects, my needs, my failures.

Right Side: Help me to see the good that you see.

Left Side: You look into my heart
and you see the real me,
not just the surface me.

Right Side: Help me to see the good that you see.

Leader (picking up the mirror from the prayer table):

I will now pass this mirror around the circle.
Look into it and as you do, silently pray:
"God, help me believe that I am good."

(Optional: After the mirror has been passed around the entire circle, invite participants to come forward to take one of the small mirrors on the prayer table as a take-

home reminder that in God's eyes each person is not just good, but very good. If you are not distributing small mirrors, continue as below.)

Silent Personal Prayer

Leader: I invite you now to spend a few minutes in silent prayer. You may move wherever you like in the room to talk to God about whatever is in your heart.

(If you have distributed mirrors, suggest that participants hold their mirrors during this prayer time as a reminder that God sees them as "very good." Allow three minutes. Then call the group together for the closing prayer.)

Group Closing Prayer

All: Thank you, God,
for the gift of ourselves.
When we want to be different:
better, smarter, stronger,
more popular, taller, shorter,
smaller, heavier, or more outgoing,
remind us that we are very, very good
just the way we are.
Remind us, too, that those around us
were created by you
and are loved by you
just the way they are.
Thank you for your gifts to others.
Thank you for your gifts to us.
Amen.

SERVICE TWO

Lost in the Crowd

Note for Leader: Moving into new groups and feeling comfortable within existing groups is a real challenge for many young adolescents. This service suggests ways they can relate to peers with love and respect. You will need a prayer table on which is placed a bible (open to 1 John, chapter one), a candle, and a basket in which there are small messages, one for each participant. The messages should be variations of these: Smile at others and they will smile at you; Reach out to others and they will respond; Always say hello first. Assign pray-ers and readers and then open the service gathered in a circle around your prayer table.

Opening Prayer

Leader: We greet you and praise you, God,
Father, Son, and Holy Spirit.
Today we want to talk to you
about fitting in and "belonging."

Pray-er One: We want to learn from you
how to get along with others.
Though many of us are in the
same groups, clubs, and classes,
or in the same band or on the same team,
we don't always feel comfortable with one another.

Pray-er Two: Sometimes we feel very alone
even in the middle of a crowd.
Help us to learn how to
love and accept one another,
and how to help one another feel
comfortable and welcome. Amen.

Scripture Reading (1 John 1:3–5 paraphrased)

Leader: *It's not easy to reach out to others, to be the first to offer love and friendship, yet in this reading Saint John encourages us to do just that.*

Reader One: What I have seen and heard
I want to tell you about now,
so that you can share God's life with me.

Reader Two: This togetherness that you and I share
comes from God the Father
and the son, Jesus Christ.
I am writing to tell you about this,
so that your joy may be complete.

Reader Three: Here then is the message
that I announce to you:
God is light and in God there is no darkness.
So let us love one another
because love comes from God.

Reader Four: The person who does not love others
really knows nothing about God,
because God is love.
The Word of the Lord.

All: Thanks be to God.

Guided Meditation

Leader: Close your eyes and slowly breathe in and out. Do this five times. ...*pause*. Now imagine that you are in a huge crowd of people. You can hardly move. You look around hoping that you'll see a friendly face, but no one looks familiar. No one is looking at you, smiling at you, or waving to you. ...*pause*.

You turn around, hoping to find an exit, but then someone grabs your sleeve. This is the person everyone has come to see! Everyone in the room turns and looks at you as this person leads you over to the food table. He invites you to help yourself and talks to you for awhile as if he knows you well. Then he leans closer and quietly tells you something personal. ...*pause*.

What he says sounds too simple to be true. You look up but the host is gone. You are alone again in the middle of the crowd, but you remember the words. You look up and catch the eye of the person next to you. You smile and the person smiles back. You look around and now everyone seems to be smiling at you. What's going on, you wonder. Why do you feel so much better? ...*pause*.

(After 20 seconds or so, invite participants to open their eyes.)

Group Response

Leader: What makes a difference for us
in the midst of a crowd?
Why do we feel so lonely at times
and then fully welcome
when someone recognizes us
and reaches out to us?

Left Side: God, you have created us
to share in your own life,
and your life is full of love.

Right Side: Teach us to reach out to others with love.

Left Side: Jesus, you have shown us
that the best love
is self-giving love.

Right Side: Teach us to reach out to others with love.

Left Side: Father, Son, and Holy Spirit,
you share a life of love and friendship.
When we feel lost in the crowd,
help us remember that we share your life
and are never really alone.

Right Side: Teach us to reach out to others with love.

All: Amen.

Silent Personal Prayer

Leader (picking up the basket from the prayer table):
I will pass this basket around the circle and I invite each of you to take one of the papers. Read what it says, and imagine that it is the message from that special person at that party—meant just for you. Spend a few minutes in silent prayer, reflecting on the message you have received. Move anywhere in the room you like.

(Allow three minutes. Then call the group together for the closing prayer.)

Group Closing Prayer

All:
Father, Son, and Holy Spirit,
teach us how to reach out to others in love.
We sometimes feel
that others should take the first step.
We wait for them to welcome us
instead of first welcoming them.
Give us the courage
to be the first to smile,
the first to say hello,
and the first to make others welcome.
Thank you for loving and greeting us,
and thank you for always being with us.
Amen.

SERVICE THREE

Life Is Not Fair

Note for Leader: Some young adolescents are outgoing and others simply are not. This service emphasizes the importance of recognizing and accepting their own particular gifts and talents. You will need a prayer table on which is placed a bible (open to 1 Corinthians), a candle, small slips of blank paper for each participant, pencils, and a basket or other container. Assign pray-ers and readers and then open the service gathered in a circle around your prayer table.

Opening Prayer

Leader: Hello, God.
We would like to talk to you today
about fairness.

Pray-er One: How can it be fair
that some of us get all the breaks
and some of us get none?

Pray-er Two: Some kids are
outgoing and friendly,
and everyone likes them.
But some are shy and quiet,
and no one even speaks to them.
How is this fair?

Pray-er Three: Why should some kids be rewarded
for what comes easy to them
while others struggle and are never rewarded?
Help us to understand this, please.
Amen.

Scripture Reading (1 Corinthians 12:4–11, paraphrased)

Leader: *You may not think that you have special gifts and talents, but indeed you do. Here Saint Paul lists some of the possibilities.*

Reader One: There are many different gifts but the same Spirit; there are different skills and talents, but it is the same God who gives them all.

Reader Two: To each person the Spirit gives gifts that will benefit the common good. To one, the Spirit gives conversational skills, to another the Spirit gives intellectual skills.

Reader Three: Through the Spirit some have a deep faith and are able to inspire others, and some have the ability to help people feel comfortable—and even to heal them.

Reader Four: But it is the one Spirit of God who produces all of these gifts, distributing them to each person as God sees fit.
The Word of the Lord.

All: Thanks be to God.

Guided Meditation

Leader: Close your eyes and slowly breathe in and out. Do this five times. ...*pause*. Now picture yourself in a waiting room, like the ones in doctor or dentist offices. There are other people in the room, but no one is talking. What are you thinking and feeling as you wait there? ...*pause*.

After what seems like forever, your name is called. You go through the door into a big bright office with windows on all sides. Someone follows you in and closes the door, a very important looking person. What are you thinking now? ... *pause*.

The person sits beside you, looks at you directly, and says, "I've been wanting to meet you for a long time. You are very important to me." The person obviously knows you well, and you feel happy and comfortable. Then she asks if there is anything you want to talk about, any concerns or problems you want to share. Say whatever is on your mind now. ...*pause.*

Before you leave, the person assures you again that you are very, very special, and she hands you a blank piece of paper. As you turn to go, she says: "You may not be all that you want to be, but remember that I like you just as you are." You think about this and you hold on to that piece of paper. ...*pause.*

(After 20 seconds or so, invite participants to open their eyes.)

Group Response

Leader: Though we don't have
official appointments with God,
God is always telling us through scripture
and through other people
that we are very special.

Right Side: God, sometimes we don't
like ourselves very much.
We wish we were more friendly and popular.

Left Side: Help us to remember, God,
that you love us as we are.

Right Side: Jesus, help us to understand
that popularity is not the only gift there is.
There are also gifts of intelligence,
musical talent, listening abilities,
understanding, athletic ability,
and many, many more.

Left Side: Help us to remember, God,
that you love us as we are.

Right Side: Holy Spirit, you are the giver of many gifts
and you give them as you see fit.
Teach us to value our own special gifts.

Left Side: Help us to remember, God,
that you love us as we are.

All: Amen.

Silent Personal Prayer

Leader (after distributing blank slips of paper and pencils):
I invite you now to write down one special talent you have, and then fold the paper in half. Spend a few minutes in silent prayer, reflecting on this talent. Move anywhere in the room you like and take the paper with you.

(Allow three minutes. Then call the group together for the closing prayer.)

Group Closing Prayer

Leader: Come forward now and place your paper in this basket.

(When all the slips of paper are in the basket hold it high.)

All: Holy Spirit,
you are the giver of all good gifts.
We may not have the exact talents we want,
but you assure us that we have the gifts
God wants us to have.
You assure us that God loves us
and values us
just as we are.
Take all our talents.
Bless them
and bless us
that we may use our gifts well.
Amen.

SERVICE FOUR

Lighten Up!

Note for Leader: Many young adolescents are uptight about everything they do and say, believing that everyone is watching and judging them. This service encourages them to be comfortable with themselves, just as God created them, so that they will be more comfortable with and accepting of others. You will need a prayer table on which is placed a bible (open to Luke, chapter 12), a candle, and small cut-out flowers, one for each participant, on which his or her name is printed. If possible, also have a vase of fresh flowers on the table. Assign pray-ers and readers and then open the service gathered in a circle around your prayer table.

Opening Prayer

Leader: Sometimes, God,
it seems like
everyone is watching us,
judging us,
waiting to make fun of
whatever we do.

Pray-er One: We need to learn from you
how we can relax
and enjoy ourselves
rather than worrying about
what other people think.

Pray-er Two: How can we
learn to be comfortable,
to concentrate on others,
and not just on ourselves?

Will you teach us how, God?
We need your help.
Amen.

Scripture Reading (Luke 12:22–31, paraphrased)

Leader: *Though it sometimes feels as if everyone
is watching us and judging us,
Jesus tells us in this reading from Luke
not to worry about such things.*

Reader One: Jesus said to his followers,
"Why do you worry so much?
Why are you so concerned about
what you will eat next,
or how you look to others,
or what clothes you should wear?

Reader Two: Living life fully
is much more important
than worrying about all these things.

Reader Three: What does all your worrying accomplish?
Does it make you any better?
Why should you be so upset
when God is taking care of you?

Reader Four: Think about the flowers growing in a field.
They don't do anything
but just be what they are,
and yet they are very beautiful.

Reader Five: Stop worrying now.
God has given you all that matters.
Have faith and only be concerned
about what God thinks of you,
and not about what others think."
The Word of the Lord.

All: Thanks be to God.

Guided Meditation

Leader: Close your eyes and concentrate on the palm of your hand. Imagine the lines and angles on it, ones that are uniquely yours, like no one else's. ...*pause*.

Imagine that one of those lines is a road. Go down it now. Soon you come to a field filled with flowers: all colors, all shapes, all sizes. Look at all the flowers for a while. ...*pause*.

You feel yourself drawn to one particular flower. You go over to it and touch it. You lean down to smell it. You have never seen such a beautiful flower. You wonder how it got so beautiful, out in this open field in the middle of nowhere. ...*pause*.

When you look up you see that someone is watching you. The person smiles and you smile back. You realize that it is Jesus. "In God's eyes, you are like that flower," he says. "You really don't have to worry about what others think of you, but I know that you do. Tell me what worries you most." Tell him now whatever is in your heart. ...*pause*.

Jesus listens carefully and then he smiles warmly at you. When he turns to go he says, "Remember, you are as wonderful in God's eyes as any flower. Don't worry so much. Enjoy yourself as you are." You look back down at that special flower. What are you thinking and feeling? ...*pause*.

(After 20 seconds or so, invite participants to open their eyes.)

Group Response

Leader: Have you ever really looked at a flower,
at all its parts, and seen
what a beautiful thing it is?
Can *we* really be so beautiful?

Right Side: We do worry too much, God.
We worry about what others will think of us
and we don't know how to relax.

Left Side: Help us to remember
that you give us everything we need.

Right Side: Jesus, you tell us that we are
more beautiful in God's eyes
than the most beautiful flower in the world.
It sounds too good to be true.

Left Side: Help us to remember
that you give us everything we need.

Right Side: Holy Spirit, be with us always,
reminding us that all that matters
is what God thinks of us.

Left Side: Help us to remember
that you give us everything we need.

All: Amen.

Silent Personal Prayer

Leader (while distributing the flowers from the table):
Here is a reminder of your conversation with Jesus in the field. Spend a few minutes in silent prayer, reflecting on this flower. It has your name on it to remind you that you are beautiful and unique in God's eyes. Move anywhere in the room you like and take your flower with you.

(Allow three minutes. Then call the group together for the closing prayer.)

Group Closing Prayer

All: Jesus, it was great talking to you.
We will try from now on not to worry so much
about what others think of us.
We will try to believe
that we are beautiful in God's eyes.
We will try to relax and enjoy
the many special gifts God has given us.
This will be hard for us
because we're so used to worrying!
So please stay near us to remind us.
Amen.

SERVICE FIVE

Everybody Does It

Note for Leader: Because peer pressure is so difficult to avoid, many young adolescents begin bad habits like smoking, drinking, or using drugs. This service emphasizes the importance of avoiding these habits and of forming good habits, in spite of what everyone else is doing. You will need a prayer table on which is placed a bible (open to 2 Corinthians, chapter 4), a candle, and a container of small prayer cards. (Make these cards beforehand using unlined index cards. On each, type or print this message: "Jesus, help us to do the right thing.") Assign pray-ers and readers and then open the service gathered in a circle around your prayer table.

Opening Prayer

Leader: Hello, God.
We need to talk to you today about choices.

Pray-er One: Sometimes we make bad choices
just to please our friends.
Sometimes we wonder:
Isn't having friends
more important than making good choices?

Pray-er Two: Don't you really expect us
to make some poor choices
while we're young?
How can it hurt to smoke or drink
if that's what it takes to belong?
If everyone is doing it,
why can't we do it, too?

Pray-er Three: We already know
the answer in our hearts, God.
It's just that it's so hard to *do* the right thing
when our friends want us to do the wrong thing.
Make us strong enough
to *always* do what's right—
no matter what.
Amen.

Scripture Reading (2 Corinthians 4:6–9, paraphrased)

Leader: *Doing the right thing is not easy,*
but Jesus is with us as we make the effort.
This reading from Saint Paul encourages us
to believe in the promises of Jesus.

Reader One: God shines in our hearts
so that we, in turn, might let others know about God.
Our bodies are fragile and weak,
and yet, we carry around in them
God's own power and presence.

Reader Two: Because of this special presence,
we do not cave in
when we are tempted to make bad choices.
We do not give up hoping that God will help us,
even when we are full of doubt.

Reader Three: Others may make fun of us,
and walk away from us,
but we know that we are never abandoned by God.
Even when others abandon us completely,
we believe that we can begin again with God's help.

Reader Four: In all our temptations and difficulties,
we must remember that we carry within us,
the life of Jesus himself.
He has promised to help us,
so that we might live
as God has called us to live.
The Word of the Lord.

All: Thanks be to God.

Guided Meditation

Leader: Close your eyes and get still enough to listen to your heartbeat. ...*pause*. Imagine that the beat is getting louder and louder and suddenly you realize that what you hear is music. You are at a school dance and noise and flashing lights are everywhere. You like to dance, but you also like to watch. What do you see right now? ...*pause*.

You feel happy just to be there, laughing, waving to friends, and watching. But then a group of kids comes up to you. You admire these kids and you would like to be one of their group. They invite you to go outside with them, and when the door chaperone turns his back, you slip out. ...*pause*.

Someone in the group tells you that they have beer and cigarettes, and they invite you to share them. You really want to. What would it hurt? You know it's not right, but you've been hoping for a chance to hang out with these kids. If you say no, they may never ask you again. You hesitate, but then you make your decision. ...*pause*. What did you decide? ...*pause*.

(After 20 seconds or so, invite participants to open their eyes.)

Group Response

Leader: Have you ever been in a situation
where you wanted something so badly
that you tried to convince yourself
that right and wrong didn't matter?
None of us can handle
such difficult situations alone.
We need God's help.

Right Side: We know the difference
between right and wrong, God,
but our friends don't always
choose what is right.

Left Side: Help us to call on you
when we feel tempted to choose what is wrong.

Right Side: Jesus, having friends means so much to us
that we often put your friendship aside.
We forget that you want only good for us.

Left Side: Help us to call on you
when we feel tempted to choose what is wrong.

Right Side: Holy Spirit, we need all the help we can get.
Help us say no when we should say no,
and yes when we should say yes.

Left Side: Help us to call on you
when we feel tempted to choose what is wrong.

All: Amen.

Silent Personal Prayer

Leader (after distributing the prayer cards):

As a reminder that Jesus is always with you, I want each of you to have one of these prayer cards. Spend a few minutes in silent prayer, reflecting on its words. Move anywhere in the room you like and take your card with you. If you want to write you own prayer on it, feel free to do so.

(Allow three minutes. Then call the group together for the closing prayer.)

Group Closing Prayer

All: Jesus, we have heard in many different ways,
that you are always with us, even in those times
when others tempt us to do the wrong thing.
We know that smoking, drinking, taking drugs,
and many of the other things
that some of our friends do,
are not the right thing to do.
and yet, we really value having friends.
We need a lot of help from you
to choose what is right,
especially in such difficult circumstances.
Please be with us always. Amen.

SERVICE SIX

A Few Good Friends

Note for Leader: Many young people abandon true friends to follow a more popular person or crowd. This service describes some of the attributes of real friendship and emphasizes the importance of valuing and affirming friends. You will need a prayer table on which is placed a bible (open to Proverbs, chapter 4), a candle, papers (on which the following two statements are printed: "The kind of friend I want to be is..." and "I think true friendship means...") pencils, and a basket or other empty container. Assign pray-ers and readers and then open the service gathered in a circle around your prayer table.

Opening Prayer

Leader: Thank you, God,
for all the gifts you have given us,
especially the gift of friends.

Pray-er One: Some of us have many friends,
and some of us have only a few.
Remind us that the numbers are not important
but that the quality of friendship is.

Pray-er Two: We need to learn how to be
loyal and generous friends,
and how to give only good example.
Those of us who are quiet and shy
need to learn how to make new friends.

Pray-er Three: Help us not to miss
the opportunities you give us
to reach out to others in love and friendship.
Thank you for loving us and believing in us. Amen.

Scripture Reading (various Proverbs, paraphrased)

Leader: *Friendship is a great gift,*
one we should never take for granted.
These passages from Proverbs praise this great gift.

Reader One: One who is a friend is always a friend,
and is like a brother or sister to us
when times get hard.

Reader Two: Some friends bring ruin on us,
but a true friend is more
loyal than our closest relatives.

Reader Three: Many try to be friends
with those who are popular or rich,
and they try to avoid those
who have nothing to give them.

Reader Four: The person who is a true friend
is always a friend, and such a one
is like a brother or sister in times of stress.

Reader Five: A good name is better
than the greatest riches,
and the esteem of friends
is better than silver or gold.

Reader Six: Do not become friends
with bad-tempered persons,
or with ones who do evil things.
You might soon imitate them
and cut yourself off
from what is right and good.
The Word of the Lord.

All: Thanks be to God.

Guided Meditation

Leader: Close your eyes and try to get perfectly still. Imagine that you are breathing *in* peace and breathing *out* worries, concerns, fears, and all negative thoughts. ...*pause*. When you feel very peaceful, picture your closest friend. What qualities make this person a good friend? What do you like best about this person? ...*pause*.

Now picture someone you would like to be friends with. What would it take to be able to call this person friend? Why do you admire him or her? ...*pause*.

Finally, picture someone who wants to be friends with you, but for whom you don't return the feeling. Why don't you want to be friends with this person? ...*pause*.

Imagine now that you are walking on a path with all three people, your best friend, someone you want to be friends with, and someone who wants your friendship. You realize as you walk that you are heading toward someone who is waiting for you. As you get closer you see that it is Jesus. He looks at you with love and understanding. He knows your feelings about the three others. He invites you to come aside to talk to him. Do so now. ...*pause*.

(After 20 seconds or so, invite participants to open their eyes.)

Group Response

Leader: Friendship is a gift
and is not necessarily something
we can feel for others or they can feel for us.
We can, however, be kind to others,
even when we don't feel close enough
to call them "friend."

Right Side: Thank you for the people
who give us the gift of friendship, God our Father,
and thank you for your love and care.

Left Side: Help us to always extend kindness
to those who care for us,
even when we can't give them
the gift of our friendship.

Right Side: Thank you for the people
who give us the gift of friendship, Jesus,

	and thank you for your love and care.
Left Side:	Help us not to compromise our values in order to win someone's friendship, even when we really want that person for a friend.
Right Side:	Thank you for the people who give us the gift of friendship, Holy Spirit, and thank you for your love and care.
Left Side:	Please give us the gifts of loyalty, concern, sympathy, and care. Help us to be the best friends we can be.
All:	Amen.

Silent Personal Prayer

Leader (while distributing the papers and pencils):
    Spend a few minutes in silent prayer, reflecting on the kind of friend you would like to be and the kind of friends you would like to have. Then complete the sentences on your paper. Move anywhere in the room you like and take your paper and pencil with you.

(Allow three minutes. Then ask participants to place their papers in the basket on the prayer table. Hold the basket high during the closing prayer.)

Group Closing Prayer

All:	God, Father, Son, and Holy Spirit, you are the example of perfect love. Help us to learn from you the meaning of true friendship. Thank you for the friends we have, and help us to be loyal and caring toward them. Give us the courage to be kind and gracious even to those we can't call friend. Always be with us to guide us. Amen.

SERVICE SEVEN

Accentuate the Positive

Note for Leader: When young adolescents compare themselves to others, they tend to focus on their negative attributes. This service reminds them that they can't be compared to anyone else because they are unique. You will need a prayer table on which is placed a bible (open to Psalm 139), a candle, and construction paper and markers. Assign pray-ers and readers and then open the service gathered in a circle around your prayer table.

Opening Prayer

Leader: To be honest, God,
we sometimes wonder who you really are.

Pray-er One: We pray to you, we go to Mass,
we hear about you in religion class,
but we wonder if you really know us
and care about us as much as people say.

Pray-er Two: We sometimes
get down on ourselves,
and it would be great to know,
that you never stop believing in us.

Pray-er Three: We don't think
we're so great sometimes;
so how can we be sure
that you care about us,
no matter what faults we have?

Pray-er Four: Could you please
give us some advice about this?
Thanks for listening, God. Amen.

Scripture Reading (Psalm 139, paraphrased)

Leader: *God knows us inside out*
and loves us no matter what.
This is the good news
proclaimed in this beautiful psalm.

Reader One: My God, you know everything about me…
you walk in front of me and behind me;
Sometimes I feel your hand resting on my shoulder.
Your loving presence seems too good to be true.

Reader Two: You always understand me,
You know every cell of my body.
You have been with me
in all that I have ever done.
And you will always be with me.

Reader Three: Your plan for me is wonderful,
more than I can grasp;
I want to trust you and believe in you,
and I always want to respond to your love.

Reader Four: If I were to fly to the farthest ends of the earth
or sail to the farthest limits of the ocean,
Your hand would still be upon me,
guiding me and holding me safe.

Reader Five: You truly know me inside out,
You even knew me in my mother's womb.
I give you thanks that I am so wonderfully made,
I praise you and thank you
for all that you have done for me.
The Word of the Lord.

All: Thanks be to God.

Guided Meditation

Leader: Close your eyes and breathe deeply in and out, in and out. ...*pause*. Concentrate on your feet and imagine that they belong to someone else. How do they hold up when you walk on them, run with them? ...*pause*.

Slowly travel from your feet up the rest of your body. Examine each part of you, remembering that God is aware of your bones, your skin, even the tiniest cells of your body. ...*pause*.

Imagine now that someone is watching you as you travel up your body from your feet to your head. You open your eyes and the person smiles at you. "What do you think," he asks, "Isn't your body incredible?" You feel embarrassed because you were thinking more about what's wrong with you. The person invites you to share what you were thinking. Take time to do that now. ...*pause*.

He listens carefully to all your concerns and seems to know just how you feel. Before leaving, he says this to you: "When you compare yourself to others, you will always come up short. Try to understand that there is no one else like you on Earth. You are unique in all the world. I love you just as you are, and I want you to know what a great gift your body is. Think about this and remember it." ...*pause*.

(After 20 seconds or so, invite participants to open their eyes.)

Group Response

Leader: All of us are tempted
to compare ourselves to others.
We do this because others judge us that way.
They compare our looks,
our athletic abilities, and our personalities
to the popular people among us.
But God judges us with love.
God sees each of us as unique and gifted.

Right Side: Can it be true, God, that you
know us so well and still love us?
Do you really know our thoughts
and all that we do?

Left Side: You know when we sit and when we stand;
you understand our thoughts before we think them.

Right Side: Jesus, you tell us in scripture
that you dwell with us
and that God dwells with us.
You must know us
better than we know ourselves.

Left Side: You know when we sit and when we stand;
you understand our thoughts before we think them.

Right Side: Holy Spirit, accepting ourselves
as we are is very hard for us.
It's so much easier to
compare ourselves to others.
Please guide us in this
because we need your help.

Left Side: You know when we sit and when we stand;
you understand our thoughts before we think them.

All: Amen.

Silent Personal Prayer

Leader (distributing the construction paper and markers):
Take time now to trace your hand or foot on this paper. *(Allow only two minutes or so for this and then call time.)* Spend a few minutes in silent prayer, reflecting on your hand or foot—or any part of your body. Move anywhere in the room you like and take your outline with you. If you want to write something on it, feel free to do so.

(Allow three minutes. Then call the group together for the closing prayer.)

Group Closing Prayer

All: Father, Son, and Holy Spirit,
We give you thanks

that we are so wonderfully made.
We praise you and thank you
for all that you have done for us.
Help us to remember
how close you are to us.
Help us to remember, too,
that all those here with us now
are special to you and unique in your eyes.
Please never stop believing in us,
and help us to believe in you.
Amen.

SERVICE EIGHT

What About Sex?

Note for Leader: Young adolescents often confuse sexuality with sexual acts. This service emphasizes sexuality as a special gift from God that helps us relate to others. It points out the difference between being a sexual person and engaging in sexual acts. You will need a prayer table on which is placed a bible (open to 1 Corinthians 6), a candle, 12" x 2" strips of colored paper, and tape. Assign pray-ers and readers and then open the service gathered in a circle around your prayer table.

Opening Prayer

Leader: God, today we want to talk to you about sex,
not sex the way our culture presents it,
as an easy give-and-take of bodies,
but as a gift from you to be treasured.

Pray-er One: We get very confused about this
because on TV and in movies
having sex with someone is no big deal.
It looks so natural and seems like fun.

Pray-er Two: But the church teaches
that having sex with someone
is only one small part
of our maleness and femaleness.

Pray-er Three: It teaches, too,
that a sexual relationship is part of the
serious commitment of marriage
in which we relate to another
with love and respect throughout our lives.

Pray-er Four: Be with us, God,
as we think about these things,
and help us to understand
what you want for us. Amen.

Scripture Reading (1 Corinthians 6:15–20, paraphrased)

Leader: *Our sexuality is one of the
great gifts God has given us.
Here Saint Paul explains why we should value it.*

Reader One: Don't you know
that your bodies belong to Christ?
Would you join the body of Christ
with someone you hardly know?
God forbid!
When you join physically with someone,
you become one flesh with them.

Reader Two: Whoever is joined to Christ
—as we are—
becomes one spirit with him.
We therefore should avoid
casual and thoughtless sexual contacts
that offend Christ and harm ourselves.

Reader Three: Don't you know that your body is
the dwelling place of the Holy Spirit?
God thinks so much of you
that you have received
the gift of God's own Spirit
to be with you always.

Reader Four: So be sure that your behavior
shows that you understand
the great gift your body is.
Always glorify God with your body
and treasure it as the dwelling place of the Spirit.
The Word of the Lord.

All: Thanks be to God.

Guided Meditation

Leader: Close your eyes and breathe deeply in and out as you slowly say three times: God is within me. ...*pause*. Think about the great mystery of God's presence. If God is within you, then God must bless every part of you, including your sexual parts. God has made you male or female with special genes and hormones. God understands all of your feelings, even your sexual feelings. Think about this for a minute. Does it seem strange to you? ...*pause*.

Picture yourself walking down a long bright hallway on your way to talk to God who is waiting for you. You sit on a bench and you ask God what you should do about sexual feelings. Imagine that God says something like this: "All of your thoughts and feelings are important to me, and everything about you has a purpose. Your sexual feelings will eventually help you to choose a partner with whom you might someday raise a family. ...*pause*.

"For now you should relate to others more simply, with affection, love, and respect, but not through sexual acts. You are not ready for a permanent commitment to another person, and you are not ready to raise a family. You are not yet ready for a sexual relationship. To have sexual feelings is natural; but to act on these feelings requires far more maturity and understanding than you now have. Trust me to help you when you are confused or tempted." Think about these words and talk to God about them. ...*pause*.

(After 20 seconds or so, invite participants to open their eyes.)

Group Response

Leader: This is a confusing time to be growing up
because our culture says
"Do whatever you feel like doing,
anytime, anywhere."
But God says "Do what is right and good,
and practice patience and self-control."
Which message is right?

Right Side: We know in our hearts
that your word is true, God;
give us the courage to do what is right.

Left Side: It's hard to understand
why we can't do what we *feel* like doing.
But your word in scripture tells us why.
We are your special dwelling places,
and our bodies are worthy of love and respect.

Right Side: We know in our hearts
that your word is true, God;
give us the courage to do what is right.

Left Side: When we are tempted to forget your presence,
when we fail to show love and respect for others,
when we are tempted to act irresponsibly,
remind us that you are with us to give us courage.

Right Side: We know in our hearts
that your word is true, God;
give us the courage to do what is right.

Left Side: Thank you for all your gifts to us
and help us to use them wisely and well.
Help us to always relate to others as you would have
us do.

All: Amen.

Silent Personal Prayer

Leader (distributing the colored strips of paper and markers):
I invite each of you to take this strip of paper and write your name on it. Your name represents all that you are and all that you feel. So let this strip remind you that God has created *every part of you* as special and good. Spend a few minutes in silent prayer, reflecting on this. Move anywhere in the room you like and take your strip with you. If you want to write something else on it, feel free to do so.

(Allow three minutes. Before the closing prayer, ask participants to twine and tape their colored strips around the person's next to them until all the strips are intertwined. Place these twined strips on your prayer table.)

Group Closing Prayer

All: You remind us, God,
that you have made us good.
You have created us to relate to one another,
but you ask us to do so wisely.
You ask us to relate to others in sexual ways,
only when we are ready
for commitment and responsibility.
Help us then to use our bodies well,
and to practice patience and self-control.
Remind us often that
at this time in our lives,
it is enough to relate to others in friendship.
Teach us how to show love and respect
for ourselves and all others,
and help us when we are tempted
to do otherwise. Amen.

SERVICE NINE

What's Wrong With Swearing?

Note for Leader: Adolescents often resort to swearing, ranking on others, and belittling others with language in order to make themselves look good. This service stresses the importance of affirming others through positive language and of avoiding the habit of swearing. You will need a prayer table on which is placed a bible (open to 1 Timothy 1:12), a candle, index cards, one for each participant, pencils or pens, and a wastebasket. Assign pray-ers and readers and then open the service gathered in a circle around your prayer table.

Opening Prayer

Leader: Hello, God,
We need to talk to you about
using your name with love and respect.

Pray-er One: We need to talk to you about
other names and words as well,
names like Jesus Christ
and words like damn, hell, and much worse.

Pray-er Two: Many of our friends
use these words to express anger,
to show off, to control others.
They don't see anything wrong with swearing,
especially if they do it to be funny
or to fit in with others.

Pray-er Three: Do you really care
how we use your name?
What does our language have to do with
how we feel about the real you?
We need guidance from you on this.
Help us please to understand what to do.
Amen.

Scripture Reading (1 Timothy 1:12–16, paraphrased)

Leader: *We are often tempted to use language*
to get control of others or to put others down.
But here, Paul tells Timothy
it just doesn't work in the end.

Reader One: I thank Christ Jesus,
who has strengthened me to be his messenger.
You see, I once swore against him,
and I persecuted those who believed in him.
I was arrogant and thought I could do no wrong.

Reader Two: I know now that I really
didn't realize what I was doing,
and so, God has been merciful to me.
God has made things more clear to me
and has strengthened me more than I can say.

Reader Three: God has now given me
a deep faith in Jesus Christ,
and it is better than anything
I have ever experienced.
You can trust my word on this
because I was once
the worst sinner of all.

Reader Four: My job now is
to guide others away from sin
and to give the best example I can.
My job now is to announce how great God is,
and how holy is God's name.
May we all give honor and glory to God,
forever and ever. Amen.
The Word of the Lord.

All: Thanks be to God.

Guided Meditation

Leader: Close your eyes and breathe deeply in and out five times. ...*pause*. Focus your attention on your head and the senses that are associated with it: your eyes that see things, your ears that hear things, your mouth that tastes things. Consider the great gift of your brain that sends messages to these parts of you. ...*pause*. Though you are made up of body parts, your brain is what really operates your body. It allows you to think about what you will do or say before you do it or say it. Think about how your brain affects the things you say *to* others or *about* others. ...*pause*.

Imagine now that you are walking down a dark hallway. It's not familiar and you feel uncomfortable. In the distance you see a woman coming toward you and she is cursing loudly. This frightens you because she doesn't seem in control. You are afraid to keep going, but there is nowhere to stop. How do you feel? ...*pause*. You close your eyes, hoping that the person will ignore you and just pass by. Suddenly the shouting stops and you open your eyes. The person is standing in front of you, looking at you. ...*pause*.

"Did I frighten you?" she asks. You nod yes. She begins to walk and talk with you. "When you swear, even to be funny, or curse at others in anger, you sound like a person out of control," she tells you. She asks you to think seriously about this and you promise that you will. You reach the end of the hall and you walk out into warm sunshine. It feels so good. As the woman tells you good-bye, she hands you a small card. "Remember," she says, "to always use your gift of speech well." ...*pause*.

(After 20 seconds or so, invite participants to open their eyes.)

Group Response

Leader: It is not just in anger
that we sometimes abuse our gift of speech.

                        Sometimes we do it just to be funny.
                        When we say "God," "Jesus Christ,"
                        damn, hell, and much worse,
                        we aren't thinking of God or Jesus at all.
                        In fact we just aren't thinking.

Right Side: Teach us, Jesus, through our words
                        to announce how great God is,
                        and how holy is God's name.

Left Side: Forgive us for the times,
                        we use your name disrespectfully, God,
                        forgive us for the times we use obscenities
                        in anger, in jest, or to put others down.

Right Side: Teach us, Jesus, through our words
                        to announce how great God is,
                        and how holy is God's name.

Left Side: Forgive us for the times
                        that we swear at our parents or friends;
                        forgive us for the times that we lose control
                        and don't stop to think about our words.

Right Side: Teach us, Jesus, through our words
                        to announce how great God is,
                        and how holy is God's name.

Left Side: Help us, loving God, to begin anew,
                        to try very hard to use our gift of speech
                        to help others, not to hurt them,
                        to raise them up, not put them down.

All: Amen.

Silent Personal Prayer

Leader (after distributing the index cards and pencils or pens):
                        I invite each of you to take this card as a reminder of your encounter with the woman in the hall. Spend a few minutes in silent prayer, reflecting on your gift of speech and how it affects others. Take your card with you and jot down a time you recently used your gift

of speech to hurt someone. Do not put your name on the card.

(Allow three minutes. Before the closing prayer, ask participants to tear up their cards and place them in the wastebasket.)

Group Closing Prayer

All: Thank you, God, for the gift of speech.
Sometimes we use it very well,
to praise, to thank,
to speak well of others.
But we also sometimes use it poorly,
to show off, to express anger,
to put others down.
Teach us how to think before we speak,
and to remember
how our words can affect others.
Forgive us for the times that we have
hurt someone with our words.
Forgive us for the times we have
cursed in anger at parents,
siblings, teachers, or friends.
Help us to believe that just as we
have torn up and thrown away
our experience of hurting someone,
so you consider it forgiven and forgotten.
May our words always
give you praise and glory.
Amen.

SERVICE TEN

Who Should We Follow?

Note for Leader: Young adolescents are under tremendous pressure today to follow people whose lives are examples of greed, immorality, and godlessness. They need people in their lives who are examples of selflessness, goodness, and faith and who live the message of Jesus. This service assures them that the message of Jesus, though difficult, is the true one. It points the way to God. You will need a prayer table on which is placed a bible (open to 2 Peter 2:1–3), a candle, a small scroll for each participant, and pencils or pens. (Make the scrolls beforehand by rolling up pieces of paper and securing them with small pieces of ribbon. The scrolls can be blank, or if you have time, print at the top of each: My Promise to God....) Assign pray-ers and readers and then open the service gathered in a circle around your prayer table.

Opening Prayer

Leader: Dear God, we know
that you love us and watch over us.
We know that you are the creator
from whom all good things come.
You sent Jesus to be among us,
to show us the way to you.

Pray-er One: The problem is, God,
the people we admire today
tell us by their lifestyles
to do only what *we* want.
They point the way to money and power,
and they don't live the message of Jesus.

Pray-er Two: These people are hard to resist,
because they are famous and successful.
We need people around us, God,
to remind us that it is Jesus we should listen to.
We need people who will
guide us and encourage us.
Send us such people, God. Amen.

Scripture Reading (2 Peter 2:1–3, paraphrased)

Leader: *In this reading, Saint Peter warns us
not to listen to those who lead us away from God.
He encourages us to be on guard against such people.*

Reader One: In times past, there were
people who led others away from God,
and today, too, there are still those among us
who are trying to convince us
to abandon God's way.

Reader Two: They even go so far
as to deny that God exists.
They make themselves into gods,
and they disregard all of God's commands.

Reader Three: They are only bringing
disaster on themselves,
and God will deal with them accordingly.
They are trying to lure others into sin,
by declaring that they know what's best,
and that they don't need God.

Reader Four: Be on your guard, then,
because these people
will surely try to deceive you
with their lies, their greed,
and their bad example.
God is very patient with them,
but I tell you for sure—
the day is coming when they will answer
for all the wicked things they have done.
The Word of the Lord.

All: Thanks be to God.

Guided Meditation

Leader: Close your eyes and try to relax. Imagine that your whole body is free of all weight, all worries, all anxiety. Picture these things floating away from your body. ...*pause*. In this completely relaxed state, picture one person whom you truly admire. What does this person look like? What does he or she do? If this person could give you one piece of advice, what do you think it would be? ...*pause*.

Imagine now that you are standing in God's presence. You can feel this presence more than see it, and it fills you with peace. God invites you to sit down to talk about your life, your goals, and the people you admire. What would you say to God about yourself? ...*pause*. What would you tell God about the people you admire? ...*pause*. What do you honestly think that God would say to you about the things you have shared? ...*pause*.

Before you leave, God invites you to come for a talk anytime. You feel very peaceful and calm about this, happy to know that God is always with you, ready to listen. You feel full of God's love and so you make a promise to God... What is your promise? ...*pause*.

(After 20 seconds or so, invite participants to open their eyes.)

Group Response

Leader: One of the hardest things, God,
is believing that you are with us.
We see rock stars, great athletes,
and television actors and actresses,
but we don't see you.
Help us to believe in your presence
because you have revealed it to us through Jesus.

Right Side: The models in our culture
teach us to live for the moment.
Jesus teaches us to live for God.

Left Side: It's really hard, God,
to resist our culture's messages:
"Buy this, get that, you need things,
you don't need God.
Have a good time, all you need is money."

Right Side: The models in our culture
teach us to live for the moment.
Jesus teaches us to live for God.

Left Side: Give us faith, please, God.
Help us to listen to those in our lives
who are trying to follow Jesus,
who are trying to find their way to you.

Right Side: The models in our culture
teach us to live for the moment.
Jesus teaches us to live for God.

All: Amen.

Silent Personal Prayer

Leader (after distributing the scrolls and pencils or pens):
I invite each of you to take this scroll as a reminder of your promise to God. Spend a few minutes in silent prayer, reflecting on it. Take your scroll with you and write out your promise. No one else will read this; it is yours to keep.

(Allow three minutes and then gather the group around the prayer table once again.)

Group Closing Prayer

All: Help us, God, to keep the
promises we have made to you.
Help us to resist the temptation

to listen to the popular people in our culture
who tell us that money is god,
and that all we really need is
clothes, jewelry, videos,
and so much more that only money can buy.
We know this isn't so,
that we really need you.
Help us to remember
that you are always with us,
even when we don't feel your presence.
Amen.

SERVICE ELEVEN

Clothes Make the Person

Note for Leader: Consumerism is one of the greatest temptations of young adolescents. Our culture, especially through the media, bombards them with the message that happiness is equal to more and more possessions. This service invites them to look around and focus on the many beautiful things they already have—especially little things—and to understand that clothes and other possessions neither offer deep happiness nor last. You will need a prayer table on which is placed a bible (open to Matthew 6:24–31), a candle, and a small container of small smooth stones, one for each participant. (If you can't get stones, substitute any small natural objects: twigs, acorns, leaves, etc.) Assign pray-ers and readers and then open the service gathered in a circle around your prayer table.

Opening Prayer

Leader: You do understand, don't you, God,
that kids can't be happy these days
unless they have a lot of clothes and other things.

Pray-er One: Our parents don't understand.
They think that we should make do
with the clothes, the jewelry, the shoes,
the haircuts, the CDs, and the computer games
that we already have.

Pray-er Two: But things keep changing so fast,
and we need to keep up—
at least we think we do.

                       Maybe that's just the problem.
                       How can we learn to feel comfortable
                       with our lives the way they are?

Pray-er Three: How can we learn to feel content
                       with the little things all around us,
                       without wanting more and more?
                       This is a real problem for us
                       and we really need your help, God.
                       Amen.

Scripture Reading (Matthew 6:24–31, paraphrased)

Leader: *Though wearing the "right" clothes*
           seems very important to us,
           Matthew says in this reading
           that God who knows and loves us,
           gives us what we need.

Reader One: Listen well to what I have to say:
                Stop worrying about how you will live,
                what you will eat or drink,
                or what you will wear.
                God will take care of you.

Reader Two: Look at the birds in the sky!
                They don't store up their food
                and yet God feeds them.
                Aren't you as important as they?

Reader Three: As far as clothes go,
                  why are you so concerned?
                  Learn a lesson from the wild flowers.
                  They don't fuss and worry about how they look,
                  and yet not even King Solomon was
                  ever dressed so beautifully.

Reader Four: If God can clothe the flowers in the field
                with this much splendor, won't God provide for you?
                Stop worrying then over what you are to wear …
                God knows all that you need.
                The Word of the Lord.

All: Thanks be to God.

Guided Meditation

Leader: Close your eyes and breathe deeply, in and out, in and out. ...*pause*. Picture yourself in an open meadow where the grass is so soft and green that you lie down on it. You look at the clouds and watch the birds that land on nearby trees. How does it feel to be seeing these things? ...*pause*.

You soon sense that another person has come into the meadow. She is watching you look at the clouds. "Aren't they beautiful?" she asks, and you agree. Then she says, "If you could have anything beautiful in your life right now, what would it be?" You think for a minute and then you tell her. ...*pause*. She asks you why you want this thing and you tell her why. ...*pause*.

She listens and you know that she really understands how you feel. "There is someone else," she tells you, "someone who understands you, no matter what, someone you can talk to any time about your wants and needs." You know in your heart that she means God. "Before you go back," she says, "talk to God for a while about the things you want, but maybe can't have. And then be still and let God speak to your heart about the beautiful things you already have." Take time to do this now. ...*pause*.

(After a minute or so, invite participants to open their eyes.)

Group Response

Leader: It's very hard for us to notice all
the thousands of little things in our lives
that are beautiful.
We're too busy and there's always so much noise.
We need to quiet down
and open our eyes to what is truly beautiful.

Right Side: Help us to believe, God,
that we don't need more things in our lives.
Help us to see the beauty all around us.

Left Side: Instead of judging people by their clothes,
their shoes, or their haircuts,
help us to notice their smiles
and to listen to what they are saying.

Right Side: Help us to believe, God,
that we don't need more things in our lives.
Help us to see the beauty all around us.

Left Side: Instead of choosing friends
based on the clothes they wear,
help us to listen to their interests and concerns
and to share and enjoy them.

Right Side: Help us to believe, God,
that we don't need more things.
Help us to see the beauty all around us.

Left Side: Thank you for all that we already have
and teach us to appreciate
what is truly beautiful in our lives.

All: Amen.

Silent Personal Prayer

Leader (after distributing the stones):
I invite each of you to take this stone (or other natural object) as a reminder of your time in the field. Spend a few minutes in silent prayer, reflecting on the beauty of this small created thing. Take it with you, examine it, and talk to God about it.

(Allow three minutes and then gather the group around the prayer table once again.)

Group Closing Prayer

All: You remind us, loving God,
that you give us many gifts,
but we forget to look for them.
Keep reminding us from now on.
Remind us that there are many beautiful things
that money can't buy.

Remind us to look at flowers and sunsets,
at heart-felt smiles and happy faces,
at birds and trees and clouds and sky,
at small smooth stones, and raindrops.
There is beauty everywhere we look.
Help us, God, to learn this hard, hard lesson
because it won't be easy
to give up our many wants and needs.
Help us to find our happiness in you.
Amen.

SERVICE TWELVE

There's a World Out There

Note for Leader: Being self-absorbed is typical for young adolescents, and thus they need encouragement to reach out to others. This service reminds them that many others around them are needy, and that they can and should reach out in love and service. You will need a prayer table on which is placed a bible (open to Matthew 25:31–46), a candle, a small garbage bag, and small slips of paper on which are written various insults, for example: You're a slob, you're ugly, you stink, no one likes you, etc. (If you have heard insults exchanged within your group, include those as well.) Assign pray-ers and readers and then open the service gathered in a circle around your prayer table.

Opening Prayer

Leader: We need to talk to you, God,
about what you want us to do
to make the world a better place.

Pray-er One: The problems are so complicated!
We can't do anything about wars and famine.
We can't get rid of poverty and hunger.
Besides we have enough trouble,
just dealing with our own problems.

Pray-er Two: And yet we know deep down
that we should be taking small steps
toward making the world a better place.

Pray-er Three: We should in some small way
be reaching out to those in need.
Help us to know what is possible for us, God,
and give us the courage and the energy
to take a first step, no matter how small.
Amen.

Scripture Reading (Matthew 25:31–46, paraphrased)

Leader: *When we feel tempted to focus only on ourselves,
this reading from Matthew
can remind us that part of being Christian
is caring for others.*

Reader One: Jesus said this to the people:
"When the Son of Man comes in glory…
all the people of the world will gather around him.
Then he will separate them into two groups,
just as a shepherd separates sheep from goats.
The sheep will be on the right
and the goats will be on the left.

Reader Two: "He will then say to those on the right:
Come, you have God's blessing;
enter the kingdom
that has been prepared for you
from the beginning of time.

Reader Three: "For I was hungry
and you gave me to eat;
I was thirsty and you gave me to drink.
I was a stranger and you welcomed me.
I was sick and you comforted me;
I was in prison and you came to visit me."

Reader Four: But they were astonished:
"When did we do these things for you?" they asked.

Reader Five: He will answer them this way:
"I assure you, as often as you did any of these things
for the least of my sisters and brothers,
You did them for me."
The Word of the Lord.

All: Thanks be to God.

Guided Meditation

Leader: Close your eyes and get still enough to hear your heartbeat. Try to block out all other sounds and concentrate only on that one sound. ...*pause*. Imagine that you are in school walking down a crowded hall between classes. You say hello when you pass those you know. You almost run into a particularly heavy girl and you say, "Move it, fatso." The kids around you laugh and you move on. Think about what you have just done. ...*pause*.

You go to your next class, feeling pretty good about how funny you are, but when you get there your teacher says the principal wants to see you. You go to the office and wait outside the door wondering what he wants. He calls you in and asks you about the incident in the hall. "The girl you insulted is my niece," he explains. "When you insulted her, you insulted me." What are you thinking now? ...*pause*.

The principal talks to you for a few minutes about the feelings of others and how important it is to respect others, especially those who aren't in your circle of friends. He explains that his niece was so upset that she went home sick. You feel pretty embarrassed about all this, and you apologize. "But the damage is done," the principal says. ...*pause*.

You slowly walk back down the hall to your class. As you go, you suddenly think: Which side would Jesus put *me* on, his left or his right? ...*pause*.

(After 20 seconds or so, invite participants to open their eyes.)

Group Response

Leader: We get so preoccupied with ourselves:
how we look to others,
what they think of us,
how funny we can be,
even at the expense of others,
that we forget to think about
those "least ones" of Jesus.

Right Side: When we make fun of others,
we usually don't mean to hurt them.
We just want
to make ourselves look better.

Left Side: I assure you, Jesus said,
what you do to the least
of my sisters and brothers,
you do to me.

Right Side: Sometimes we're the ones
who get made fun of,
and it doesn't seem so funny.
It hurts not to be accepted
—just as we are.

Left Side: I assure you, Jesus said,
what you do to the least
of my sisters and brothers,
you do to me.

Right Side: We forget so easily
that others have feelings.
We don't look past
our own thoughts and plans.
We have to remember
the teaching of Jesus.

Left Side: I assure you, Jesus said,
what you do to the least
of my sisters and brothers,
you do to me.

All: Amen.

Silent Personal Prayer

Leader (after distributing the "insult" slips):
I invite each of you to take this piece of paper as a reminder of your talk with the principal. Spend time now in silent prayer, reflecting on what the paper says and how you would feel if someone said the words to you. Take it with you and talk to God about it.

(Allow three minutes and then gather the group around the prayer table once again. Before saying the closing prayer, have participants tear the slips in half and throw them in the garbage bag.)

Group Closing Prayer

All: Jesus, you are very clear about
how we will someday be judged:
not by the wise and clever things we have said,
not by the number of friends we have had,
or how popular we were,
or by the expensive things we possessed,
or even by the talents we were given.
No, we will be judged on love.
All you will want to know is:
How well did we love and respect others?
How well did we reach out to them,
and share ourselves with them?
It's so simple and yet so hard.
Please take all the insults
we have ever thrown at others,
and forgive us for having said them.
Amen.

SERVICE THIRTEEN

Why Parents Make You Do It

Note for Leader: Because young adolescents face so many obstacles and struggles, they need spiritual guidance and nourishment. This service points out how the Mass, sacraments, and other forms of church ritual prayer can strengthen and guide them. You will need a prayer table on which is placed a bible (open to Luke 22:19–20), a candle, and a loaf of bread (fresh baked, if possible). Assign pray-ers and readers and then open the service gathered in a circle around your prayer table.

Opening Prayer

Leader: We need to talk to you, God,
about the ways we praise and worship you.
We need to think about
Mass and the sacraments
and why these are important ways
to be in touch with you.

Pray-er One: Our parents say that it's
very important that we go to
Mass and receive the sacraments,
and they make us do these things.

Pray-er Two: Why can't we just pray to you
in private in our rooms at home?
Why does the church want us
to go to Mass week after week?

Pray-er Three: The words and the prayers
all seem so monotonous to us,
and the scripture readings
are from so long ago.
Why are these things important God?
Please let us know. Amen.

Scripture Reading (Luke 22:19–20, paraphrased)

Leader: *Jesus is always there for us,
offering us spiritual food and drink.
When we celebrate the Mass and the sacraments,
we remember him in a very special way—
as this reading from Luke tells us.*

Reader One: When the hour arrived,
Jesus took his place at the table
with his friends gathered around him.

Reader Two: He said to them:
"I have really wanted
to share this meal with you
before I suffer and die."

Reader Three: Then, taking the bread
and giving thanks, he broke it
and gave it to them, saying:
"This is my body to be given for you.
Every time you eat it, remember me."

Reader Four: He did the same
with the cup of wine after eating,
saying as he did so:
"This cup is the new covenant in my blood.
Whenever you drink from it, remember me."
The Word of the Lord.

All: Thanks be to God.

Guided Meditation

Leader: Close your eyes and breathe deeply, in and out, in and out. Think of a place deep within yourself that is your central place, your core. Let your mind go to that place and rest there a moment. ...*pause.*

Imagine now that something great has happened in your life. Maybe you got a great report card, or scored a touchdown, or got a great part in the school play. What's the first thing you do when something good happens? Very likely you call a friend or gather somewhere with him or her. Perhaps you tell your family members and they share your joy in some special way. Think about this for a minute. ...*pause.*

Imagine now that you are facing something very difficult...*pause.* Perhaps you failed a test, or missed a touchdown, or didn't get picked for the school play. Or maybe something even worse has happened. What do you do? With whom do you share this difficulty? ...*pause.*

Because we are human, we need to share our experiences, both good and bad, with others. The same is true of our religious experiences. The church recognizes that we can best keep the memory of Jesus alive and follow his teachings by gathering weekly at Mass and by praying together at other significant moments of our lives. Think about this for a moment. ...*pause.*

(After 20 seconds or so, invite participants to open their eyes. As they are reciting the group response, ask an adult helper to break the bread into small pieces, one for each participant.)

Group Response

Leader: Jesus, deep in our hearts
we know that religious ceremonies
are very important in our lives.
They remind us that you are always with us
pointing the way to God.

Right Side: When we are tempted
not to go to Mass, not to pray,
and not to receive the sacraments,
remind us of our need for you.

Left Side: It is through these experiences

           that we encounter you in a special way.
           As a community of believers,
           we express our faith with you in our midst.

Right Side: Help us to remember that
           we, too, have something to offer
           every time we go to Mass.
           We can reach out to those around us
           and share our faith and our prayers.

Left Side: This is very hard for us, Jesus,
           because we like to be entertained.
           The Mass can be hard work,
           too hard unless you help us.

Right Side: Above all, help us to remember
           that every time we gather at Mass,
           every time we pray together,
           we do it to remember you.

All: Amen.

Silent Personal Prayer

Leader (after distributing pieces of the bread):
           I invite each of you to take this piece of bread as a reminder that when we break it together at Mass Jesus is with us in a special way. Hold it as you now spend a few minutes in silent prayer.

           (Allow three minutes and then gather the group around the prayer table once again. Before saying the closing prayer, have participants eat the bread.)

Group Closing Prayer

Leader: Together let us pray
           a slightly different version of the Our Father,
           a prayer Jesus taught us,
           and which we pray at every Mass.

All: Our Father in heaven,
           your name is great and we praise you.
           Help us—by the way we live—

to make your kingdom present here and now.
Help us to always do
what you ask of us,
just as the saints and angels do in heaven.
Give us and all your children
the food and drink we need today.
Forgive us for our sins
in the same way that we forgive those
who have wronged us.
Help us not to give in to temptation,
and keep us safe from every kind of evil.
Amen.

SERVICE FOURTEEN

Is There Really a God?

Note for Leader: Even young adolescents who actively practice their faith have nagging doubts about God. This service encourages them to believe—without proof—that God, through and in Jesus, is always with them to guide and strengthen them in the growing-up process. You will need a prayer table on which is placed a bible (open to John 20:24–29), a candle, and cut-out cardboard crosses, one for each participant. Assign pray-ers and readers and then open the service gathered in a circle around your prayer table.

Opening Prayer

Leader: We believe in you, loving God,
but sometimes we wonder about life
and faith and your presence in our lives.

Pray-er One: At school and with friends
no one talks much about you.
On TV people never go to church
or pray or talk about you,
except to be funny.

Pray-er Two: Our culture tells us
that if we have money, we don't need God.
Even in church people don't seem to believe,
really believe, that you are in their lives.

Pray-er Three: Where can we find answers
to our questions about you, God?
Please give us the gift of faith. Amen.

Scripture Reading (John 20:24–29, paraphrased)

Leader: *God asks us to believe in Jesus*
—even without proof of his presence.
In this reading, we see what happened to Thomas
when he did not believe.

Reader One: It happened that Thomas,
one of the twelve apostles, was absent
when Jesus came to offer them
peace and forgiveness.
The others told Thomas about it,
but he refused to believe,
and he even demanded proof.

Reader Two: A week later,
the disciples were once again gathered,
and this time Thomas was there.
"Peace be with you," Jesus said.
Then he looked at Thomas.
"Take your finger and examine my hands.
See the wounds there (from the crucifixion).
You must no longer doubt that I am alive."

Reader Three: Thomas was clearly embarrassed.
He cried out this prayer of belief
in response to the words of Jesus:
"My Lord and my God," he said.

Reader Four: Jesus then said to Thomas,
"You only believe that I rose from the dead
because you have seen me.
Blessed are those who have not seen me
and yet have believed."
The Word of the Lord.

All: Thanks be to God.

Guided Meditation

Leader: Close your eyes and focus your attention on the palm of your hand. Look at the lines. Imagine that you are following one of those lines. ...*pause*. It leads to a room where a heated discussion is taking place. It soon becomes obvious to you that these people are Christians and they are arguing about how best to share their message with others. One of them looks at you and asks you to join in the discussion. What will you say? ...*pause*.

A young woman in the group speaks up. She says she wants to believe in God and in Jesus, but that she finds it hard. She says that she doesn't see any evidence. Someone answers her: "Sometimes faith means believing without any evidence, but sometimes we just don't look around to *see* the evidence. When we love one another and care for those in need, God is at work among us. When even two or three of us gather in his name, Jesus promised to be among us." You listen carefully to all of this and you think about it for a minute. ...*pause*.

But then the young woman speaks up again, "You mean I will never know for certain that God exists?" Someone answers, "Maybe not, except deep in your heart. Remember what Jesus said to Thomas: 'Blessed are those who have not seen and yet have believed'." The young woman says she will think about these things. Why don't you, too, take time now to think about your *own* faith and even your doubts. ...*pause*.

(After 20 seconds or so, invite participants to open their eyes.)

Group Response

Leader: Sometimes we don't see
the signs of your presence, loving God,
because we don't look around us
to see the good works done in your name.

Right Side: Blessed are those
who have not seen
and yet have believed in me.

Left Side: Sometimes we don't hear
your voice, Jesus, because we don't
take time to quiet down and listen.

Right Side: Blessed are those
who have not seen
and yet have believed in me.

Left Side: Sometimes we are like Thomas,
Holy Spirit of God,
We want to touch you,
to *feel* your presence.

Right Side: Blessed are those
who have not seen
and yet have believed in me.

All: Amen.

Silent Personal Prayer

Leader (after distributing the crosses):
Take this cross as a sign of your Christian faith. Hold it as you now spend a few minutes in silent prayer, talking to God about your doubts and your beliefs.

(Allow three minutes and then gather the group around the prayer table once again. Before the closing prayer, invite participants to write something they believe on one side of the cross, and a doubt they have on the other.)

Group Closing Prayer

All: Loving God, Jesus Christ, Holy Spirit,
we come before you like Thomas,
doubting your presence and asking for signs.
Help us to understand
that *we* are the signs of your presence
when we love one another,
serve the needy, and gather in your name.
Teach us how to do this, loving God. Amen.

APPENDIX ONE

Get-Acquainted Activities

As I mentioned in the Introduction, it can be very beneficial to do a get-acquainted or "icebreaking" activity with children before you invite them to pray together. This is especially important in groups where the children come from different schools or neighborhoods and do not know one another well. It's also important, however, even for children who do know one another because it helps them relax and relate to one another in a lighthearted way before sharing prayer. There are, of course, many games you can play to help children get acquainted, but because time is limited in most religion classes, I will describe here two of the simplest types of activities.

Circle Activities

Among the easiest activities are circle games. You simply invite participants to gather in a circle and take turns introducing themselves or saying something about themselves. You might also consider the following variations.

• Have one child begin by introducing him or herself and naming his or her favorite food. (If you're doing this in religion class, you might want to use topics from your lesson, for example, name your favorite sacrament, saint, prayer, etc.). Then the next person introduces him or herself, names a favorite food, and then repeats the name and favorite food of the first person. Each succeeding person must introduce everyone who has gone before. This gets very funny after four or five people because there are so many names to remember. Children really listen hard and try to remember names, so this is a very effective get-acquainted exercise.

• Another variation is to give directions and ask everyone to follow them silently while remaining in the circle. For example, say:

Turn to the person on your right and shake hands.
Turn to the person on your left and shake hands.
Slowly turn around two times.

Put your hands on your hips and slowly move backward five paces.
Put your hands on your shoulders and slowly move forward five paces.
Move to the right ten paces.
Move to the left ten paces.
Reverently and dramatically make the Sign of the Cross.
Fold your hands and bow deeply.

•A third variation is to form two circles with equal numbers of children in them, an inner circle and an outer circle. Children in the inner circle should face outward, and each person in the outer circle should be facing someone in the inside circle. Explain that you will be asking them to share something, and after they do so, you will call out "switch" and the children in the outside circle will move to the right, thus facing a new person. The object of this circle game is to move quickly so participants can share information spontaneously with everyone in the group. You can give any directions you like, for example:

Share with your partner your full name (switch), your favorite color (switch), your worst subject in school (switch), the last movie you saw (switch), and so on.

If doing this in religion class, use religious directions, for example: Share with your partner the name of one of the apostles, your favorite prayer, one of the sacraments, a part of the Mass, etc.

Autograph Activities

These exercises involve paper and pencils and sometimes designated questions. The simplest autograph activity involves giving children two minutes to collect the signatures of everyone in the group, but again consider the variations:

•Have children also get "information" from everyone. For example, in addition to each person's signature, each should also write his or her favorite book, movie, TV show, video, etc.

•Another variation is to have children get opinions from four people in the group and take notes on these for later sharing. For example, they might ask the four people: What is your opinion of church music? or, When is the last time you saw someone being baptized (married, confirmed, etc.)? They must really listen in order to take notes, and they often learn quite a bit about the other children in the process.

•A third variation is to have children interview one other person in the group with questions supplied by you. These should be pre-printed to save time, and if done during religion class, they can be questions about your lesson. This is a very interesting way to test religion knowledge and/or to review.

When you do brief get-acquainted activities like these, children will not only learn about one another, but they will begin to look forward to your class and to the prayer experiences they share with one another.

APPENDIX TWO

Preparing for Guided Meditation

Because many children have not had experience with meditation or with guided meditation as part of their prayer, you might want to do warm-up exercises with them before you actually lead them in prayer. For example, invite them to spend a few minutes in any given class getting quiet by using one or more of the following directions. Always move from the simplest to the more complex.

1. Close your eyes and be silent.
(You'll be amazed at how hard this first step is for many. There will be giggling, snide remarks, and many, many open eyes. Be patient and calm and don't go on until all have closed their eyes and are perfectly quiet.)

2. Slowly breathe in and out, listening to your breath. Do this five times.
(Again, many will open their eyes to see if others are following this direction, so gently repeat the first direction as well as the second.)

3. Listen to your heart beat. Let your mind focus on it—and on it alone. Put all other thoughts or feelings aside.
(Some in your group might still be uncomfortable, but do persist. Don't tolerate noise or interruptions—but reprimand offenders gently.)

4. Now imagine that all your worries, your troubles, your problems are flowing away from your body. Try to picture them leaving. If a problem or worry comes to your mind, let go of it, let it flow away from you.
(In this fourth step you are getting closer to introducing God into this time of quiet. Be sure that all present are taking this time seriously before you make it a time for prayer.)

Reprinted with permission from *Prayer Services for Young Adolescents* by Gwen Costello
© 1994 Twenty-Third Publications, P.O. Box 180, Mystic, CT 06355 (800-321-0411).

5. Imagine God's peace and love flowing into you. All of your worries and concerns have left your body. Try to feel God's peace and love flowing in and let it calm you. If problems or concerns come to your mind, put them aside and only focus on the peace and love that have taken their place.

(When your group has reached the point of being able to follow your directions through all five steps, you are now ready to use the guided meditations in this book.)

Before You Begin

The following guidelines will be helpful to you, especially if you have never led children in this form of prayer.

- Always read a guided meditation through completely (before you use it with children) so that you are well aware of its direction.

- Practice reading it slowly and reflectively. Read it aloud several times. Read it dramatically but prayerfully. Practice until you feel comfortable. If you are embarrassed, your group will sense this and will also feel uncomfortable and embarrassed.

- Introduce the guided meditations in the book as written, or first use the five steps above. You know your own group best. They may need more lead-in time than is offered in the prayer services.

- Allow sufficient pauses during a guided meditation. If you sense that your group needs less pausing, adapt accordingly. If they seem to need or want more pauses, insert them where they seem appropriate to you.

- Allow at least 20 seconds at the end of each meditation for participants to bring it to a close in their own minds and hearts.

- Do not discuss the meditation or their response to it until after the Closing Prayer. Then *invite* comments, but do not force them. This is, after all, an experience of personal prayer and should be shared willingly, if at all.

Also by Gwen Costello...

Praying with Children
28 Prayer Services for Various Occasions
The prayer services here cover the seasons of the year, liturgical feasts and special occasions. For teachers, catechists and parents.

ISBN: 0-89622-439-2, 96 pp, $9.95

Prayer Services for Religious Educators
Here are 32 prayer services that beautifully address areas such as liturgical feasts, contemporary concerns, and other faith topics useful to prayer leaders. The services are brief, yet deeply inspiring.

ISBN: 0-89622-390-6, 82 pp, $9.95

Reconciliation Services for Children
18 Prayer Services to Celebrate God's Forgiveness
The 18 ready-to-use services in this book help set the tone for kids in grades 2-6 to receive the sacrament of reconciliation.

ISBN: 0-89622-516-x, 80 pp, $9.95

A Bible Way of the Cross for Children
A Scripture-based stations of the cross that invites participation, reflection and prayer. For ages 7-12.

ISBN: 0-89622-353-1, 32 pp, $1.95

Stations of the Cross for Teenagers
Fifteen "personalized" reflections on Jesus' journey to Calvary with meditations that relate to real-life situations of teenagers.

ISBN: 0-89622-386-8, 32 pp, $1.95

Leading Children to God
This four-part audio program is for catechists, DREs and all who work with children and teenagers in catechetical settings. While the main focus is on helping children build a relationship with God, listeners are challenged to examine their own habits of communicating with God

Two 35-minute audiocassettes, $16.95

Available at religious bookstores or from

TWENTY-THIRD PUBLICATIONS
P.O. Box 180 • Mystic, CT 06355
1-800-321-0411